HOW TO LIVE IN
HEALTH
AND
WHOLENESS

PRINCIPLES FOR HEALTH & WHOLENESS
IN BODY, SOUL AND SPIRIT

HOW TO LIVE IN
HEALTH
AND
WHOLENESS

PRINCIPLES FOR HEALTH & WHOLENESS
IN BODY, SOUL AND SPIRIT

BRIAN HOUSTON

PUBLISHED BY MAXIMISED LEADERSHIP

DEDICATION

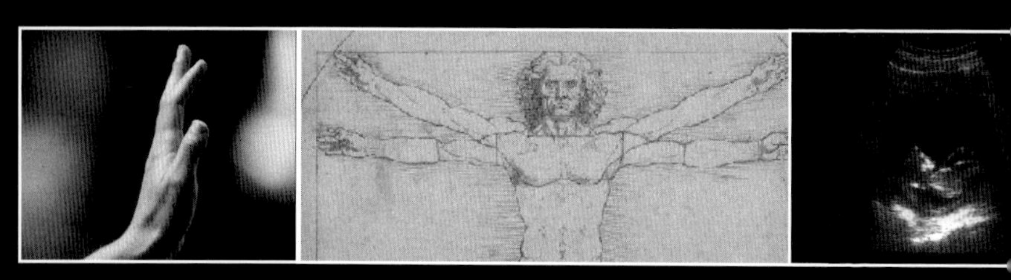

They are life to those who fi

\HEALTH\, n. [OE. helthe]

hale, sound, whole. [See ‘whole’.] The state

of being hale, sound, or whole, in body, mind,

or soul; especially, the state of being free from

physical disease or pain.

[Source: Webster's Revised Unabridged Dictionary]

health

em, and health to all their flesh.

Proverbs 4:22 [NKJV]

health

Give attention
to my words ...
for they are life to
those who find them,
and **health**
to all their flesh.

[Proverbs 4:20,22]

HOW TO LIVE IN HEALTH

Health is a gift from God. A great and sometimes, underestimated gift from God. Good health has been a very real friend to God's plans and purposes for my life. Undoubtedly, this is why the Apostle John of the New Testament, declared 'prosperity and good health' to be his greatest wish for his good friend, Gaius.

Do you believe good health is God's will for your life? I most definitely do! My first experience of healing was at the age of six. My mother heard strange noises coming from my bedroom and ran in to find me unconscious and blue. The doctor came urgently and suggested that, without improvement, I should be transferred by ambulance to the hospital. He was so concerned that he came twice more during the night, but my parents prayed fervently, and trusted God. To the family doctor's amazement, the following morning I woke up and told my father I was 'starving,' and asked for the Weet-Bix, before running outside to play.

Time and again, over the years I have seen God's hand of healing in people's lives.

How much value do you place on your health and well-being? There are a multitude of resources available on the subject of health, including materials on diet, exercise, spiritual healing, medical advice and natural alternatives. I am sure these vary in effectiveness, but I believe the foundational keys we require to live a healthy life are contained in one book – the Bible. God's will for you is health and He has given you a comprehensive manual, filled with His Divine wisdom for health and wholeness. God's promise is this:

'Give attention to my words; incline your ear to my sayings ... for they are life to those who find them, and health to all their flesh.'

[Proverbs 4:20,22 NKJV]

I would imagine that the greatest gift you could offer someone struggling with sickness or pain is their health. My hope is that this book will help you discover Bible principles that will help you live the way that God intended: in health and wholeness!

creation

I will praise
You
for I am
fearfully and
wonderfully
made.

[Psalm 139:14]

The first chapter of the Bible declares that God made you and me in His own image. Knowing this helps us to understand why David expressed his gratitude to the Creator by saying:

'I will praise You, for I am fearfully and wonderfully made. Marvellous are Your Works, O Lord...' [Psalm 139:14 NKJV]

I have often joked that Bobbie, my wife, is 'wonderfully' made, and me? Well, I'm 'fearfully' made! I certainly do know that God's handiwork is marvellous. He used His own image as the blueprint in creating us. Imagine that! We are made in the image of a God of three distinct yet interconnected parts – Father, Son, and Holy Spirit. Similarly, He made us in three inseparable parts – body, soul, and spirit.

Each part has the potential to impact the others either positively or negatively. Medical science recognises that pain or injury in one area can significantly impact the other two areas. Research has found emotional or psychological problems can result in physical symptoms, and vice versa. In the same way, I believe what we face spiritually can also be outworked physically and emotionally. Don't underestimate the impact your health can have on the quality of your life. Remember, you are alive to serve God and poor health can stifle your capacity to do so.

The dictionary defines health in terms of wholeness in body, mind, or soul. It goes beyond the physical and this holistic approach embraces every aspect of our lives, including building healthy relationships and healthy attitudes.

Throughout the centuries, artists and sculptors have attempted to capture the wonder of the human body, and we live at a time where people aspire to physical perfection. This causes many to worship the creation rather than the Creator. In the 21st century, genetic scientists are attempting to clone what God originally designed, yet they can only fall short of the workmanship of the Master craftsman. As the psalmist writes:

'It is He who has made us, and not we ourselves.' [Psalm 100:3 NKJV]

Made in His image, the human body was created to function effectively in perfect health and in a perfect environment. That was before the fall when Man became separated from God. But the work of Jesus on the Cross reversed the curse, and because of Him, we can live in health and wholeness today.

stripes

But He was wounded for our transgressions, He was bruised for our iniquities; The chastisement for our peace was upon Him, and by **His stripes** we are **healed.**

[Isaiah 53:5]

The life of Jesus Christ has been depicted many times in art, music and literature, but Mel Gibson's movie '*The Passion of the Christ*' stands out as one of the most graphic and deeply impacting portrayal of the hours leading up to Jesus' death. The Gospel of John clearly stated the purpose:

> '*For God so loved the world that He gave His only begotten Son , that whosoever believes in Him should not perish but have everlasting **life**.*' [John 3:16 NKJV]

The Crucifixion is the most significant act of love the world has ever seen, yet so many never fully grasp what Jesus did for us then. Many believers understand that He died for our sins so we could have eternal life, but the work of the Cross also purchased wholeness and healing for our physical life on earth. Centuries before Christ's death, the prophet Isaiah wrote:

> '*He was wounded for our transgressions, He was bruised for our iniquities; The chastisement for our peace was upon Him, and **by His stripes we are healed**.*' [Isaiah 53:5 NKJV]

The Roman custom of scourging prisoners involved a whip with one or more lashes which often had pieces of wire or sharp bone attached to each strand. As each lash tore at His flesh, the stripes on the body of Jesus were for the healing of us all.

Isaiah's words are powerful: 'By His stripes, we are healed.' It doesn't refer to healing in the past (i.e. we *were* healed) but it is written in the present tense, declaring we *are* healed – physically, emotionally and spiritually!

During His earthly life, Jesus encountered many who were sick and healed them. The Bible says:

> '*And great multitudes followed Him, and **He healed them all**.*'
>
> [Matthew 12:15 NKJV]

Yet healing was not limited to the touch of Jesus 2,000 years ago. On the Cross, Jesus paid the price for the greatest antidote to ill-health and brokenness for us today.

life

I have come that they may have **life,** and that they may have it **more** abundantly.

[John 10:10]

'Loving God, loving people, loving life' is one of the defining themes of Hillsong Church. It expresses our personal passion to build a *healthy* church full of *healthy* people who have a *healthy* relationship with God.

Visitors to our church often remark on the spirit of life that prevails there. 'It is so positive,' some are heard to say. This particularly stands out to those whose perception of church is a place that is dead and lifeless. Sadly, there are some churches that were once thriving places of worship but have degenerated to a state of ill-health. Somewhere along the line they began to lose the spark of life.

The analogy between the Church and a human body is scriptural, yet the 'body of Christ' was never meant to represent a dead, lifeless corpse. Instead, we should reflect a body that is pulsating with life, energy and creativity – the image of the very source of life Himself.

Jesus is synonymous with life. Everything about Him points towards healing and wholeness but there are some who blame God for their ill-health. I have never found scripture that says His will for us is sickness. On the contrary, Jesus said:

*'The thief does not come except to steal, and to kill, and to destroy. I have come that they may have **life**, and that they may have it more abundantly.'* [John 10:10 NKJV]

The elements of an abundant life don't include suffering or sickness. Death and destruction is the desire of the devil. Jesus referred to him as a 'thief' and he will always try to rob us of the life God intends for us.

During our lives, we will find ourselves facing the health hazards the devil throws our way. These could be attacks against our physical bodies, emotions, relationships, and even our churches.

The good news is that God has ensured that we are well equipped and positioned to win. The Bible provides us with the wisdom we need to sustain health and life across the spectrum of our lives

The Sun of Righteousness shall **aris**

HEALING

1. To restore to health or soundness; cure.

2. To set right; repair.

3. To restore (a person) to spiritual wholeness.

healing

ith healing in His wings   [Malachi 4:2 NKJV]

healing

For I am the Lord who heals you.

[Exodus 15:26]

I have been preaching, teaching, or pastoring for over thirty years now. During that time I have seen how a person's belief shapes their reality.

God's will for us to be in health is opposed by the devil's goal to keep us contained through sickness and suffering. Unfortunately, some people accept beliefs about God and sickness that simply are not true. They end up living at the level of their belief and never know the fullness of God's blessing.

It saddens me when suffering people are told their illness is God's will because He wants to teach them a lesson, or that sickness is a result of 'sin in their life'. If that were true, we would all be dead, because we are all sinners! I have met people who were told they weren't healed because they 'didn't have enough faith'. Such 'diagnoses' replace hope with hopelessness, guilt or condemnation.

The book of Job tells of his darkest days. In a time of great suffering, he was surrounded by well-intentioned friends who really were more of a hindrance than a help. One said there must be something wrong with Job or 'God would have healed him by now.' Another told Job to accept his suffering as 'God's will.'

After 41 chapters, and with much discussion and dialogue among these so-called 'comforters', Job finally concluded:

'I know that You can do everything and that no purpose of Yours can be withheld from You.' [Job 42:2 NKJV]

The outcome was that God restored Job's health and he was granted twice as much as he had before. He went on to live to a ripe old age and *'the Lord blessed his latter days more than his beginning'* [Job 42:12].

A foundational key to good health is a revelation that God is our healer. Instead of lowering your beliefs to the level of your experience, I encourage you to rise above circumstances and stand firm on your beliefs. No matter what the outcome, believe and trust Him when He says:

'I am the Lord who heals you.' [Exodus 15:26 NKJV]

weapons

For the weapons of our warfare are not carnal but mighty in God.

[2 Corinthians 10:3]

EQUIPPED FOR HEALTH

One certainty about life is that we will face challenges. It could be a fight for our health, a battle in our minds, or even contending for our spiritual well-being.

In these times we need to have the spirit of an overcomer rather than be overwhelmed or ruled by our situation. This involves a determination to rise up and take hold of what is rightfully ours.

The Apostle Paul used the analogy of a war:

'For though we walk in the flesh, we do not war according to the flesh. For the weapons of our warfare are not carnal but mighty in God for pulling down strongholds.' [2 Corinthians 10:3,4 NKJV]

When doing battle for our health, there are spiritual weapons readily available to us. The greatest of these is prayer. Prayer has the power to change circumstances and situations. James wrote:

'Pray for one another that you may be healed. The effective fervent prayer of a righteous man avails much.' [James 5:16 NKJV]

Prayer changes things. A study of the life of Jesus will reveal that prayer was the source of His strength. When facing any major situation, Jesus would take time to pray. For example, in the Garden of Gethsemane before He was arrested, Jesus steeled Himself in prayer to physically endure the Cross.

The Lord has provided the means for our healing in many different ways and on various levels. In my own experience, I have witnessed God's healing power numerous times through each of the following:

1. Nature
2. Medicine
3. Faith
4. Miracles

In the following chapters, we will examine each of these and see how we can gain His promise of health and wholeness in our own lives.

nature

You made

all the delicate,

inner parts of my body

and

knit me

together in my

mother's womb.

[Psalm 139:13]

Like every adventurous young boy, I had my share of accidents and injuries while growing up – broken toes, broken fingers and I even broke an ankle whilst tobogganing on a sheet of corrugated iron! Remarkably though, today I am still in one piece. Wounds that needed stitching (and a trip to the casualty ward) have healed; torn muscles and broken bones have knitted together. The Bible says:

> *'For You formed my inward parts; you knit me together in my mother's womb.'* [Psalm 139:13 NKJV, NIV]

God created the human body with the ability to heal and repair itself. I believe this is one of the ways God has made provision for our health and healing. Our immune system is designed to naturally counteract the effects of sickness or injury. You don't have to think about it – your body naturally works towards health and healing.

The Ancient Greek physician, Hippocrates, observed this too. He said:

> *'Natural forces within us are the true healers of disease.'*

The capacity of the human body to recover is certainly remarkable but don't leave your physical health to chance. We live on a planet which is governed by natural laws, such as the law of gravity. You know, what goes up, must come down. As we get older, the impact of gravity on our ageing bodies becomes more and more obvious.

Then there is the second law of thermodynamics, or the law of entropy, which states that everything is proceeding toward a state of greater disorder or decay. Left to their own devices, our physical bodies inevitably tend towards decay.

Friend, if you don't manage your health, you may end up managing a health crisis. Unfortunately, you can only do so much about the natural ageing process, but if you will invest into your own well-being (body, soul and spirit), the best years of your life may be well ahead of you. Be encouraged by the words of the Apostle Paul:

> *'Therefore we do not lose heart. Even though our outward man is perishing, yet the inward man is being renewed day by day.'*
>
> [2 Corinthians 4:16 NKJV]

medicine

Those who are
well have no
need of a
physician
but those
who are sick.

[Luke 5:31]

A doctor named Luke wrote one of the most detailed accounts of Christ's life and ministry. I find it interesting that a man whose profession involved healing felt so compelled to research and document the life of history's Greatest Healer. Luke wrote in his Gospel:

'Jesus answered and said to them, "Those who are well have no need of a physician, but those who are sick."' [Luke 5:31 NKJV]

I have no problem believing that God can use medical professionals to heal us because that is what God does – He uses people. He doesn't have to, but He chooses to. He can use people to minister life and health to you in the same way that He uses people to establish His Church on the earth.

Some see modern medicine as a contradiction to their faith, but I don't believe this is so. A doctor's diagnosis or prescription has saved many a life, and let us not forget Jesus' stated purpose: He came to give us life, both now and in eternity.

Five centuries before the birth of Christ, Hippocrates radically influenced popular medical beliefs. Up until that time, the main cause of illness was considered to be demonic possession or evil spirits, but Hippocrates introduced a scientific approach. His main emphasis was to build up a patient's strength through diet and hygiene. While the Bible does cite demons as responsible for certain conditions, it is obviously not always the case. Often, a practical approach to health is what is needed.

The Hippocratic Oath still sets the ethical standards for medical practitioners today. Hippocrates wasn't a Christian but he recognised there was a spiritual side to healing. He wrote:

'Prayer indeed is good, but while calling on the gods a man should himself lend a hand.' [Hippocrates, *Regimen*]

Thank God for dedicated people who have studied medicine and devoted their lives to alleviating or healing the pain of others. They are helping people enjoy what God intended for them – health and wholeness.

faith

Your
faith
has made
you well.

[Luke 17:19]

Have you ever received a negative health report? It can certainly come as a shock, but how you respond is all important. This is where faith gets involved. You have the diagnosis but now, what are you going to believe? Despite a bad report, you can still believe that God's will for your life is health and wholeness.

Faith is so important in the pursuit of supernatural healing. Our church, Hillsong Church, is committed to praying for the sick. We believe through faith in God, people can be healed. The Bible makes this clear:

*'The prayer of **faith** will heal the sick, and the Lord will raise him up.'* [James 5:15 NKJV]

Every week we receive praise reports and testimonies from those whose prayers have been answered. If someone isn't healed in the way we expect, I am not going stop believing God's Word, the Bible. Bringing our belief down to the level of our experience will never help. We should do exactly the opposite. Commit to lifting your experience to the level of your belief!

Some cynics would say that encouraging faith in God for healing is giving people 'false hope', but I believe *some* hope is better than no hope at all. Even the secular proverb professes, 'Where there is life, there is hope!'

Faith connects you with God's will for your life. Jesus made the following statement on several occasions:

*'Your **faith** has made you well.'* [Matthew 9:22; Mark 10:52; Luke 17:19 NKJV]

When He healed blind Bartimaeus, the woman haemmoraging blood and one of ten lepers, Jesus remarked on their faith. He also marvelled at the faith of a Roman centurion who believed his servant would be healed and spoke of *'such great faith'* [Matthew 8:10].

Your faith is crucial to health and healing, but it must never become an issue of guilt or condemnation. Christians should never judge another's level of faith. To say that a lack of faith prevented someone's healing is a judgmental and ungodly attitude. Rather than judging or preaching at sick people, our love and compassion should shine through. We should *'rejoice with those who rejoice, and weep with those who weep'* [Romans 12:15].

miracles

Power
went out from
Him
and He healed
them all.

[Luke 6:19]

There is something deep within humanity that is fascinated by the supernatural. The Book of Luke describes multitudes flocking to Jesus because news had spread of His miraculous works.

*'And the whole multitude sought to touch Him, for **power** went out from Him and healed them all.'* [Luke 6:19 NKJV]

We live in a world that craves instant gratification. When we get sick, we want an immediate cure. Amazingly, people desire the miraculous; yet struggle to accept the God of miracles in their day-to-day lives. Some theologians and churchgoers believe miracles were performed through Jesus and the Apostles in Bible times. They may also believe in a supernatural here-after. They just don't believe that God is still doing miracles today, and I think that is tragic!

A miracle is an event that 'appears inexplicable by the laws of nature and so is held to be supernatural in origin or an act of God' [Dictionary reference]. It is a force that works above the laws and limitations of nature. A miracle occurs when God speeds up the process of time or accomplishes what is naturally impossible. Without doubt, miracles reveal God's supernatural intervention and they bring glory to Him.

We may be limited by the confines of the physical, natural world but through Him, we can experience the supernatural in every aspect of our lives.

The work of the Cross brings supernatural healing. Not only can we obtain physical healing from sickness and disease, but broken hearts are healed; as are broken relationships, emotions and even finances.

We serve a God of miracles, and believing in Him means we must believe it all. That is, all His promises, which are ours because of the death and resurrection of Jesus.

I believe God is able to perform supernatural miracles in your life. No matter what challenges you are facing, never forget that the Bible states:

'For with God nothing will be impossible.' [Luke 1:37 NKJV]

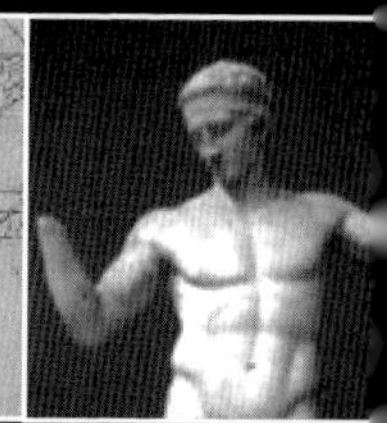

His ruling authority will grow,
and there'll be no limits t

\Whole"ness\, n.

The quality or state of being whole,

entire, or so sound; entireness; totality;

completeness.

[Source: Webster's Revised Unabridged Dictionary]

wholeness

he wholeness he brings. [Isaiah 9:7 MSG]

whole

Do you want to be made whole?

[John 5:6]

With wholeness comes change. A person who is physically whole can walk, run, jump or skip. To be emotionally whole means you can love, forgive, speak positively and have hope. Spiritual wholeness signifies you are changing, growing, and are positioned to live life purposefully.

Some 2,000 years ago, Jesus encountered a man who had been an invalid for 38 years. He spent his days lying next to the pool of Bethesda in Jerusalem, hoping for a miracle. At certain times, it was believed an angel would stir up the water and the first person in the pool would be cured of their disease. On meeting this man, Jesus asked:

'Do you want to be made whole?' [John 5:6 KJV]

What a strange question! This man had had that condition for 38 years and Jesus asked him if he wanted to be made whole! Perhaps the question was about more than physical healing. I can't help but think what Jesus was ultimately asking was this: 'Do you want to be complete? Do you really know what wholeness will mean, and the responsibility it will bring?'

Think about it. It is not easy to change after 38 years in a certain condition. The fact is, if you go through life with a limp, you have a reason not to attempt a 100 metre sprint, let alone train for a marathon.

The moment Jesus told the man to 'rise up and walk,' his life was about to change. There was no reason for him to return to the pool the next day. Everything would be different.

While people may think they want to be made whole, many don't want the responsibility and accountability that goes with it.

Wholeness for an abused person means they are ready to forgive and move on. For a hurt person, it means they are ready to trust again.

'Do you want to be made whole?'

The question is as relevant to us today as it was back at the pool of Bethesda. Are you willing to accept the changes or make the adjustments in all areas of life that wholeness may demand?

complete

He who has begun a **good** **work** in you will **complete** it until the day of Jesus Christ.

[Philippians 1:6]

Imagine spending hours completing a jigsaw puzzle, only to discover that there is one piece missing. What stands out – the beautiful picture or the one missing piece?

Like this jigsaw puzzle, it is often one small, unresolved issue that prevents us from reaching our full potential and living life, whole.

Take the person blessed with good looks and natural talent but blighted by insecurity. They have everything they need to succeed in life, but somehow fall short of the mark. Insecurity or a low self-esteem could be the missing piece – the limitation that sabotages their personality and affects their communication, relationships, and their sense of self worth. Ultimately this one 'missing piece' can swamp all the good qualities they are naturally blessed with.

The Apostle Paul encourages us to keep growing and expanding:
*'Being confident of this very thing, that He who has begun a good work in you will **complete** it.'* [Philippians 1:6 NKJV]

The desire to be whole and complete in body, soul and spirit should be within each of us. The Bible describes believers as 'living epistles' – people watch us because we reflect the image of the Creator. If you bought a car and it didn't function properly, it wouldn't reflect well on the manufacturer. When our lives are moving toward wholeness, it reflects well on our Maker.

Being whole means we can enjoy the abundant life Jesus spoke about. To know the fullness of life He promised, we should be willing to be accountable and take responsibility.

Being whole is not just about us and our needs. When we are whole, we have the capacity to help or lift up others, and they can depend on us.

So, do you want to be made whole?

Christ wants to deal with the real issues in your life so you can move forward. Instead of a band-aid mentality to Christianity, we need to allow the Holy Spirit to reveal those areas that limit us, and begin a work that will enable us to become all that God has called us to be.

soul

I pray that you may

prosper in

all things and be in

health, just as

your **soul**

prospers.

[3 John 2]

soul

One of my greatest priorities as a pastor is the on-going health of our church. You see, I have learned over the years that attacks from the outside don't hurt us and ultimately don't determine the well-being of the church. If the soul of our church is healthy, weapons may be formed against us but they will not prosper. The reality is that a healthy body is impacted by a healthy soul. The Apostle John wrote:

'Beloved, I pray that you may prosper in all things and be in health, just as your soul prospers.' [3 John 2 NKJV]

I believe there is a direct correlation between the condition of our soul and our overall health. What is happening on the inside affects what is on the outside.

The soul is like the engine room of our lives. It is the seat of our thinking, emotions and will. When the core of our being (our soul) is unhealthy, it has a significant effect on everything else.

In many of the psalms, it is evident that the writer recognised the importance of the condition of his soul. When he felt distressed on the inside, he would speak to his inner man.

'Why are you cast down, O my soul? And why are you disquieted within me? Hope in God; for I shall yet praise Him, the help of my countenance and my God.' [Psalm 42:11 NKJV]

These words paint a picture of someone who refuses to be dictated to by unproductive feelings, negative thoughts or poor internal choices. He took command over his own soul and pointed his own inner world toward hope.

Do you want to be made whole?

Take a look at the words of John:

'Dear friend, I am praying that all is well with you and that your body is as healthy as I know your soul is.' [3 John 2 NLT]

Don't neglect the health of your soul because it is a foundational key for a healthy life.

heart

My **heart** also

instructs me in the night

seasons.

[Psalm 16:7]

If it is the content of our hearts that determines the condition of our lives, surely we must dig beneath the veneer and ask ourselves the tough questions. What is really happening within me? And, what am I prepared to do about it?

Here is a Proverb with some clear advice:

'*For as* [a man] *thinks in his heart, so is he.*' [Proverbs 23:7 NKJV]

Human nature tends to react to external things, rather than dealing with the inner issues. The devil is crafty and attempts to defeat us on the inside. He wants to attack our source of strength. The Bible says:

'*The spirit of a man will sustain him in sickness, but who can bear a broken spirit?*' [Proverbs 18:14 NKJV]

When something is broken, it doesn't function properly. If you are broken on the inside, you won't be in a strong position to withstand attacks. If you are serious about living a life of wholeness, you will give attention to the real issues of your heart.

Life will throw some 'night seasons' your way and during these times we will be directed by our hearts. David wrote:

'*My heart also instructs me in the night seasons.*' [Psalm 16:7 NKJV]

Many things breed in the dark including confusion or disorientation. You can lose your way in the darkness of night and have no clue which way to turn. I have seen people completely lose their way during dark or difficult times, and others who have emerged victoriously. Why do some make it through?

When you don't know which way to turn, your heart is going to guide you; and it can only instruct according to what it knows. If your heart is geared toward panic, it will guide you accordingly, whereas, with the right thinking and attitudes, your heart can keep you on course. Just as a plane flies according to the way its computer is set, our lives will fly according to the way our hearts are set. Sadly, some people lose their way in a night season and never find their way back.

Do you want to be made whole?

Perhaps the key lies in the content of your own heart.

inside

Marvellous
are Your works,
and that my
soul
knows
very well.

[Psalm 139:14]

Personal trainers can help you change the condition of your physical body but how can you change the condition of your soul? It will take some commitment and discipline, but here are five ways you can begin to build health on the inside.

1. Teach your soul when to be quiet

'My soul, wait silently for God alone.' [Psalm 62:5 NKJV]

Many conflicting voices can dictate what happens on the inside. King David was always quick to silence other voices by instructing his soul to focus on the Lord. He commanded 'everything within him' to bless the Lord. He was telling every conflicting emotion to be quiet!

2. Educate your soul

'It is not good for a soul to be without knowledge.' [Proverbs 19:2 NKJV]

Some pursue intellectual knowledge in order to build their lives, but fail to see the value of educating their soul. You can have degrees or doctorates but ultimately, it is what your soul knows that will direct the course of your life – positively or negatively!

3. Fill your soul with hope

'This hope we have as an anchor of the soul, both sure and steadfast.'
[Hebrews 6:19 NKJV]

Without hope, we have nothing to anchor or secure ourselves to when we are tossed by the storms of life. Those consumed by despair and hopelessness find themselves unhinged and then quickly drift off course. You can keep hope alive and strong by daily meditating on God's Word.

4. Teach your soul to boast

'My soul shall make its boast in the Lord.' [Psalm 34:2 NKJV]

Those who need to boast about themselves display all the evidence of insecurity. You can develop a different type of boast though, by 'boasting in the Lord': 'How good is God?' or 'My hope is in the name of the Lord!'

5. Teach your soul to be accountable

Blaming others or our circumstances is typical of human nature. Excuses only give us reason to stay the way we are. Building a healthy soul starts with accepting responsibility and accountability for our own lives.

And the Lord our God commanded us to obe
for our own p

well-being

these laws and to fear Him

perity and well-being [Deut 6:24 NLT]

priority

Like fish
taken in a
net,
like birds
caught in a
snare.

[Ecclesiastes 9:12]

God has blessed me with good health! Without it, I doubt I could have done all I have been able to do during more than 30 years of ministry. I receive many invitations from churches and conferences all over the world. With the rigours of constant international travel, the challenge of leading a large staff, church, college and movement, you can imagine that my health has been essential.

Health should be our priority when we are well, not only when we are sick. Prevention is better than cure. It makes sense to look after ourselves rather than sap our strength struggling with ongoing health issues.

The Bible says:

'... like fish taken in a cruel net, like birds caught in a snare, so the sons of men are snared in an evil time, when it falls suddenly upon them.' [Ecclesiastes 9:12 NKJV]

Instead of swimming with ease the way God intended, a fish caught in a net will use all its energy and resources to attempt to break free. It is the same for a bird caught in a snare. It flaps itself to exhaustion with the hope of flying again. Sadly, we can spend a lot of energy and resource trying to regain our health. Human nature means we are inclined to take good health for granted until we lose it.

Making good health a priority is not vanity. In the context of living with God-given purpose, health is a commitment to longevity and effectiveness. This is why we need to keep in good shape. If the devil can inhibit us physically, or lead us into a depressed emotional state, he will. Avoiding his snares puts us in a much stronger position to help others.

Those who get emotionally entangled in various situations can end up needing help themselves. Determine to break free of the nets and snares that could potentially ensnare you, in order to live life fully and effectively. In the words of Jesus:

'If the Son sets you free, you will indeed be free.' [John 8:36 NLT]

free

If the Son
sets you
free,
you will
indeed be
free.

[John 8:36]

Sickness seems to strike randomly and it is certainly not based on what we deserve. There are various reasons why we fall ill. Statistics suggest that 38 per cent of all cancers are related to diet and lifestyle. Some would believe it is more.

Undoubtedly, poor attitudes and negative emotions are key contributors to ill-health. Deep-seated anxiety, grief or resentment often results in severe physical consequences. There is evidence that some ailments have direct links to unforgiveness or bitterness, while stress can also have severe repercussions. The Bible warns:

*'looking carefully ... lest any **root of bitterness** springing up cause trouble, and by this many become defiled.'* [Hebrews 12:15 NKJV]

Unresolved negative emotions will have an adverse affect on your general well-being. Trouble is the result of unforgiveness. It will punish *you*, not the perpetrator or the cause of your pain. The writer to the Hebrews was well aware of the destruction that a hardened heart can bring. He wrote:

'Do not harden your hearts as in the rebellion in the day of trial in the wilderness.' [Hebrews 3:8 NKJV]

A hard heart locks out God, locks out others, refuses to trust, and cannot be penetrated. It is no longer theory that our emotions can affect our health. It is a medical fact. It is crucial that you deal with bitterness at its roots and maintain a free, or unblocked, spirit. The Apostle Paul said:

'"Be angry, and do not sin", do not let the sun go down on your wrath.' [Ephesians 4:26 NKJV]

The key is to deal immediately with the issues that confront you. Every time the sun goes down in the evening, it will rise again in the morning. If it sets on unresolved issues, it will carry them into a new day. For some people, the sun is completely shaded by yesterday's 'stuff.' They are living with the physical, emotional or spiritual fallout of years of unchecked emotions. I have chosen not to allow unproductive emotions to fester or put their roots down in my spirit. I encourage you to do the same. Choose to forgive in order to live free from bondage, brokenness and ill-health.

peace

Be
anxious
for nothing.

[Philippians 4:6]

Have you ever heard anyone claim they were sick with worry? Perhaps this is closer to the truth than many people realise. I once taught a series of messages called, 'What a worry, worry is!' – and it is! Anxiety is a genuine health hazard. It dulls the senses, destroys objectivity and can affect you physically, emotionally and spiritually. The Bible warns us of the consequences of worry in the inner man:

'*Anxiety in the heart of man causes depression.*' [Proverbs 12:25 NKJV]

We can allow our minds to take us down a path of negative possibilities. Everything becomes magnified, perspective is lost and we start focusing on worst case scenarios. There is nothing to be gained by this. When depression pervades the heart, it affects your whole outlook on life. Another proverb says:

'*Hope deferred makes the heart sick.*' [Proverbs 13:12 NKJV]

We know that the issues of life spring from the heart, and that a sick heart will have ramifications on our general well-being. To tackle this, we need to take on God's thinking. He says:

'*For I know the thoughts I think toward you, says the Lord, thoughts of peace and not of evil, to give you a future and a hope.*' [Jeremiah 29:11]

It is in the midst of a challenge that you find out whether you really trust Him with your future. There have been occasions when I have found myself worrying more than could be deemed healthy. I felt the effects in my neck and back, and have even lost my voice because of it.

Worrying is about trusting in your own ability. The Apostle Paul tells us how to respond to anxiety:

'*Be anxious for nothing, but in everything by prayer and supplication, with thanksgiving, let your requests be made known to God; and the peace of God, which surpasses all understanding, will guard your hearts and minds through Christ Jesus.*' [Philippians 4:6,7 NKJV]

The key is to turn worry into thanksgiving. The Bible doesn't tell us to thank Him *for* everything but to give thanks *in* everything. In the midst of a worrying situation, find something to thank Him for. Replace anxiety with that internal peace that surpasses all understanding. God's peace is like a mental guard or protective shield for your heart.

laugh

A merry
heart does
good,
like medicine.

[Proverbs 17:22]

How many senses do you have? Five? Let a hearty sense of humour become the sixth! We can take life far too seriously, but there is nothing like a belly laugh to lift the spirits and give a healthy perspective on life.

The Bible speaks of humour as one of life's greatest medications:

'A merry heart does good, like medicine, but a broken spirit dries the bones.' [Proverbs 17:22 NKJV]

Another translation says,

'A cheerful disposition is good for your health.' [Prov 17:22 The Message]

Research has proven this to be true. Not only is a cheerful spirit good for your health, but it also impacts your surroundings. A house filled with laughter will be a *healthy* home; a great sense of humour in a relationship will aid a *healthy* marriage; and a congregation with a merry heart is a sign of a *healthy* church.

I have often said that church should be enjoyed, not endured. Sadly, some churches, take themselves far too seriously. I believe that Christians should be the happiest of all people – and maybe the funniest! The life and soul of the party.

Psalm 100:2 has been a key verse in the culture of our church. It says:

'Serve the Lord with gladness.' [Psalm 100:2 NKJV]

This refers to our spirit and attitude, and for good reason – a merry heart enables us to serve Him with greater energy and health.

American author Mark Twain recognised the power of laughter when he said:

'The human race has one really effective weapon, and that is laughter.' [Mark Twain]

A free and happy spirit will impact the quality of your life and help you ride through the tough times. Weapons may be formed against our health and well-being, but we can fight back with a merry heart. My motto is 'love God, love people, and love life.'

'Happy are the people whose God is the Lord!' [Psalm 144:15 NKJV]

overcome

In the world you will
have tribulation;
but be of good cheer,
I have **overcome**
the world.

[John 16:33]

DEALING WITH DEPENDENCIES

An unexpected blessing that has come from pastoring Hillsong Church, is the opportunity to be an unofficial 'chaplain' and friend to some key people in sport, entertainment and other high-profile roles. It has given me insight into the pressures, temptations and demands that come with a public profile. Unfortunately, history tells of many in similar positions who shattered incredible opportunities through excess or unhealthy dependencies because they didn't have the right foundation.

We all face challenges in life, and we too can become trapped in a cycle of excess or dependency in an attempt to cope. The public fallout may be greater for people of profile but the toll on our well-being is the same, regardless of who we are.

When the going gets tough, where do you turn to? We were created to be dependent beings – dependent on a loving God as our source of strength, rather than in bondage to addictions. The Bible says:

*'**Trust** in the Lord with all your heart, and **lean** not on your own understanding...'* [Proverbs 3:5 NKJV]

Human nature is more inclined towards being 'in-dependent' or relying on our own strength instead of leaning on Him. Sadly, it is pursuits outside God's parameters that can develop into destructive dependencies. The result is addictions or obsessive behaviour that can overshadow every sphere of life.

The Bible describes the body as a 'temple of the Holy Spirit'. You cannot abuse your physical body and expect to function effectively through the journey of life. In a way, we are all like elite athletes running a race. The Apostle Paul used this analogy:

'Do you not know that those who run in a race all run, but one receives the prize? Run in such a way that you may obtain it. And everyone who competes for the prize is temperate in all things ...' [1 Cor 9:24,25 NKJV]

Do you have temptations or weaknesses with the potential to rob you of your prize? If the prize is measured in health, happiness, family, friends, and successfully fulfilling God's will for your life, you need to challenge, starve or cut off any excess or dependency that threatens them. Do whatever it takes! The only dependency that will ultimately breathe life into your health and well-being is dependency on the Lord Jesus Christ.

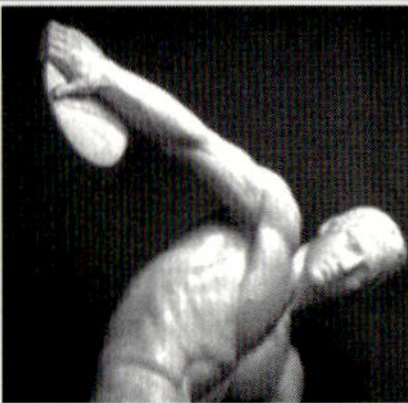

Do you know how the clouds are

balance

BALANCE

The state of being in equipoise:

equilibrium; even adjustment;

balance

...nd poised in the heavens], the wonderful
works of Him Who is perfect in knowledge?

[Job 37:16 AMP]

source

Eat

honey

because it is good,

and the honeycomb

which is sweet to

your taste.

[Proverbs 24:13]

I don't believe the Bible is the strict book of rules and regulations that many believe it to be. With a New Testament perspective, we view the scriptures according to all that Christ has accomplished. And He has set us up to win!

Life is best when you make wise and positive choices. These are choices which are based on the teachings of Jesus. I don't think my role as a pastor is to tell people what to do and what not to do. I want to equip them to make their own positive decisions – and the best decisions are geared toward producing positive outcomes in every area of life.

We need to be mindful that both health and harm can come from the same source. Look at this analogy of honey from the book of Proverbs:

'My son, eat honey because it is good, and the honeycomb which is sweet to your taste' [Proverbs 24:13 NKJV]

We know that honey is good and it tastes good. But one chapter later there is a caution:

'Have you found honey? Eat only as much as you need, lest you be filled with it and vomit.' [Proverbs 25:16 NKJV]

Now I'm not aware that honey appears on any list of banned substances, but Solomon is clearly encouraging restraint. He is teaching that too much of a good thing can harm us. Health and moderation are partners.

Understanding that health and harm come from the same honey-jar should alert us to the need for discipline and balance. A healthy, Christ-like lifestyle is not so much abstinence-based as it is wisdom-based. The Apostle Paul understood the need for balance:

'Everything is permissible (allowable and lawful) for me; but not all things are helpful (good for me to do, expedient and profitable when considered with other things). Everything is lawful for me, but I will not become the slave of anything or be brought under its power.'
[1 Corinthians 6:12 AMP]

We all have strengths and weaknesses, and it is up to us to take responsibility for our own well-being. Don't allow someone else's conviction (or lack of it) to become your downfall; and don't make lifestyle choices without regard for their impact on others.

balance

The **spirit** indeed is

willing, but the
flesh

is weak.

[Matthew 26:41]

To live your life saying 'yes' to God and 'no' to sin is a recipe for good health!

'Fear the Lord and depart from evil. It will be health to your flesh, and strength to your bones.' [Proverbs 3:7,8 NKJV]

What we sow determines what we reap. I have already stated that the responsibility rests with us to make good choices. Solomon's proverb on honey encourages us to set positive boundaries for our lives. What does Solomon's 'honey' represent in your life? Excessiveness has been the ruin of many. Often, a bit of self-discipline and common sense would have prevented things from spinning out of control.

If you know you have a weakness for something, don't put yourself in an environment where such things are in abundance. This is why the company we keep is important. The Bible says:

'Bad company corrupts good habits.' [1 Corinthians 15:33 NKJV]

Jesus told His disciples:

'Watch and pray, lest you enter into temptation. The spirit indeed is willing, but the flesh is weak.' [Matthew 26:41 NKJV]

There is a constant battle between the flesh and the spirit, and our everyday choices are contributing to one or the other. Decide you are not going to feed your weaknesses. Draw some responsible boundary lines in your relationships and across your life. Such parameters are releasing, rather than restricting, as they will promote good health.

We all face different challenges and some things are a matter of personal taste and choice. What is tempting to you may not be tempting to me. The scriptures are filled with principles that will help you build a healthy life. The key is to be true to yourself. Live life with conviction and avoid falling into the traps of excess and obsession. As the proverb states:

'Have you found honey? Eat only as much as you need.' [Proverbs 25:16]

Don't judge others. Remember, the Bible has as much to say about gluttony as it does about drunkenness. Moderation does not only apply to one area but should be applied across the spectrum of our lives. Don't over-indulge. Health and harm come from the same honey-jar!

food

For the Kingdom of God is not about **food** **and drink**, but righteousness, peace and joy in the Holy Ghost.

[Romans 14:17]

In recent times, a lawsuit was brought against a large fast food chain in America. The complainant wanted financial compensation for years of eating their 'junk' food that he claimed resulted in obesity and subsequent health problems. The case was ultimately dismissed by the judge, who declared it was not the place of the law to protect people from their own excesses.

Taking responsibility for our choices includes what we eat and drink. We all need to fuel our bodies to function properly, but an unhealthy attitude to food or drink can be destructive. Some people turn to food to give them a pick-up when they are depressed, and others rely on alcohol to boost their poor self-image or low self-esteem. The Bible warns us about the consequences of these type of excesses:

'For the drunkard and the glutton will come to poverty' [Proverbs 23:21]

It is interesting that on many occasions the scriptures speak of wine-bibbing and gluttony in the same sentence. Excessiveness in any form causes harm. At Hillsong Church, we don't impose rules about what people eat or what they drink; but we do teach the importance of moderation and wisdom.

The Bible has plenty to say about the things we consume, and the Old Testament contained numerous dietary laws. Jesus gives us a New Covenant which liberates us from regulations but, of course, that doesn't mean we should abandon wisdom. The Apostle Paul brought proper perspective:

'For the Kingdom of God is not about food and drink, but righteousness, peace and joy in the Holy Ghost.' [Romans 14:17 NKJV]

In the early Church, some of the Jewish believers held their dietary traditions in higher regard than accepting Gentiles into the Church. Their focus was more on regulations than on God's Kingdom. Jesus said:

*'Do not worry about your life, what you will **eat** or what you will **drink**; nor about your body, what you will put on. Is not life more than food and the body more than clothing?'* [Matthew 6:25 NKJV]

He went on to instruct us to seek first the Kingdom and His righteousness. To live a healthy life, we need to exercise caution and focus on the things that matter. Health and harm come from the same honey-jar!

exercise

Do you
not know that your
body is the temple
of the Holy Spirit who
is in you?

[1 Corinthians 6:19]

It's never easy to get out of bed in the middle of winter, pull on those trackpants and jog a few kilometres in the cold morning air. But it always feels good to have done it!

We live in a society that is extremely image conscious. We need to look after ourselves – body, soul and spirit – and a healthy attitude to exercise is both valuable and necessary. But of course, obsession is never healthy and balance is essential. The Bible says:

'Do you not know that your body is the temple of the Holy Spirit who is in you... ?' [1 Corinthians 6:19 NKJV]

Our bodies need to be kept in good shape to function well. How can we fulfill the purposes of God in our lives if we neglect our bodies? There is a Spanish proverb that says:

'A man too busy to take care of his health is like a mechanic too busy to take care of his tools.'

Your body is the vehicle God has given you to carry out His purposes. He has a great plan for your life and you need to be in good health to fulfill it. You don't need your body to break down halfway into your journey. The Apostle Paul recognised this:

'But I discipline my body and bring it into subjection ...'
[1 Corinthians 9:27 NKJV]

Looking after your body will add to your health and well-being. I know that I do everything better when I exercise and endeavour to be physically fit. But the honey-jar principle applies here too. Don't allow exercise and image to become an obsession that unbalances or rules your life. Paul wrote:

*'For **bodily exercise** profits a little, but **godliness** is profitable for all things, having promise of the life that now is and of that which is to come.'* [1 Timothy 4:8 NKJV]

Paul wasn't dismissing exercise. He acknowledged its benefits but he put into perspective the area most people tend to neglect – the spiritual side of their lives. Remember to exercise those spiritual muscles as well. Health and harm come from the same honey-jar!

sex

Flee
sexual
immorality.

[1 Corinthians 6:18]

sex

The Bible presents a different moral code to the worldly lifestyle. Some may mock these principles and call them old-fashioned, but they simply give us healthy parameters in order to live life well. These parameters are not there to limit or suppress our lives but rather to bring blessing.

Sexual intimacy is a wonderful God-given gift, and it has the potential to enhance a loving relationship. Yet outside Godly principles, it can bring heartache, devastation, mistrust and brokenness.

Remember the scripture says that health and harm come from the same honey-jar. There are many who have been devastated by the abuse of uncontrolled sexuality. What God intended to be healthy and beautiful is perverted. Trust can be broken, emotions scarred, relationships devastated, and futures affected – all because of immorality.

The Bible clearly indicates the perils of sexual immorality, using the analogy of a woman who is inviting and alluring:

'For the lips of an immoral woman drip honey.' [Proverbs 5:3 NKJV]

This chapter of Proverbs continues to illustrate the destruction of promiscuity. Many are quickly captivated and seduced by the sweetness of the moment, without contemplating the disastrous results at the end of the road. They end up paying a massive personal cost. The Apostle Paul said:

'Flee sexual immorality.' [1 Corinthians 6:18 NKJV]

His strong counsel is to run from sexual temptation. We are not taught to resist temptation – we are taught to flee from it. Don't even put yourself in a compromising position, physically or emotionally. This includes guarding your mind from the sexual images that are subtly promoted in the media. You need to know when to switch off ... without delay!

Sex is good, but not when we ignore God's counsel. Marriage was His idea and is the perfect fit for a healthy sex life.

Health and harm come from the same honey-jar!

rest

I lay
down and
slept;
I awoke,
for the Lord
sustained me.

[Psalm 3:5]

rest

The Carpenters sang, 'Rainy days and Mondays always get me down' but that's not true for me! I love Mondays. It's my day off. After multiple weekend services, expending much physical, emotional and spiritual energy, I am ready for a quiet Monday.

In the first chapter of Genesis, we are told that God Himself rested on the seventh day. To live a healthy, balanced life we need to know the value of rest. A good night's sleep equips us to serve the Lord effectively. It's His way of renewing, restoring and replenishing us. We can only keep going a certain amount of time before we lose our concentration and edge. That is, of course, unless we rest! The promise of God is this:

'When you lie down, you will not be afraid. Yes, you will lie down and your sleep will be sweet.' [Proverbs 3:24 NKJV]

Like rest and relaxation, our sleep should be a sweet reward, not ridden with fear and anxiety. I love the way in the midst of increased opposition, David was able to say:

'I lay down and slept; I awoke, for the Lord sustained me.' [Psalm 3:5]

I lay down! I slept! I awoke! This sounds better than tossing and turning all night, then waking up ragged and exhausted. I believe for this blessing in my life. It was a good night's sleep that renewed David's strength for the challenges of a new day, but his son, Solomon, warns us against becoming sluggish. Sleep is a reward for a hard days work, yet, for some, work is an unwelcome interruption to their sleep.

'Do not love sleep, lest you come to poverty.' [Proverbs 20:13 NKJV]

Some people are asleep to their potential and they miss opportunities to serve God. Life is for living, not sleeping. I love my Mondays, but their value is achieved by approaching the rest of the week with a zest for work and accomplishment. The purpose of sleep and relaxation is to re-charge us so we can live effective, purpose-filled lives. It is important to find the balance. Jesus said, *'Come to Me all you who **labour** and are heavily laden, and I will give you **rest'*** [Matthew 11:28 NKJV].

He spoke of work and rest in the same sentence, and ultimately the two should complement one another. Don't be striving so hard that you forget to enjoy life. In the midst of the busyness of life, we need to know when to stop and rest.

longevity

With

long life

I will satisfy him, and

show him My

salvation.

[Psalm 91:16]

LEADING A HEALTHY EXAMPLE

Undoubtedly, leadership is example. It is all about giving people something to follow. As a Church leader, I want my leadership to be seen in my marriage, my family, my finances, and across all other areas of my life.

A leader's attitude is critical in sickness and in health. My wife Bobbie and I have recently watched on, as several of our close friends have confronted life threatening illnesses. Their faith and their courage have been awe-inspiring. Sometimes, it is in these very real challenges that true leadership is proven. I am committed to last the distance and to fulfill everything that God has called me to do.

We all need to make our health a priority. The promise of God is this:

'With **long life** I will satisfy him, and show him My salvation.'

[Psalm 91:16 NKJV]

The devil will attempt to attack your physical, mental and spiritual well-being because he wants to render you ineffective. The truth is that if you don't manage your health, you may find yourself trying to manage a health crisis, and you don't want that!

God has given us everything needed to live life well. Through the Bible, we are given the wisdom and instruction by which we can develop a positive and productive attitude to health and wholeness. A genuinely biblical approach to health is not legalistic. With Godly wisdom, and with good parameters in place, you can enhance your well-being. I believe in divine health – Bible principles produce Bible results!

My closing prayer for you echoes the words of the Apostle John:

'I pray for good fortune in everything you do, and **for your good health** –that your everyday affairs prosper, as well as your soul!'

[3 John 2 The Message]

Life is for living, so live it well.

The best is yet to come!